The Wright Brothers

by Lola M. Schaefer

Consulting Editor: Gail Saunders-Smith, Ph.D.

Consultant: Darrell Collins, Historian,
Wright Brothers National Memorial,
National Park Service

Pebble Books

an imprint of Capstone Press
Mankato, Minnesota

Pebble Books are published by Capstone Press
151 Good Counsel Drive, P.O. Box 669, Mankato, Minnesota 56002
http://www.capstone-press.com

1 2 3 4 5 6 05 04 03 02 01 00

Library of Congress Cataloging-in-Publication Data
Schaefer, Lola M., 1950–
    The Wright brothers/by Lola M. Schaefer.
    p. cm.—(Famous people in transportation)
    Includes bibliographical references and index.
    Summary: Simple text and photographs present the lives of Wilbur and Orville
Wright and their pioneering efforts in the development of the airplane.
    ISBN 0-7368-0549-4
    1. Wright, Orville, 1871–1948—Juvenile literature. 2. Wright, Wilbur,
1867–1912—Juvenile literature. 3. Aeronautics—United States—Biography—
Juvenile literature. [1. Wright, Orville, 1871–1948. 2. Wright, Wilbur, 1867–1912.
3. Aeronautics—Biography.] I. Title. II. Series.
TL540.W7 S33   2000
629.13′0092′2—dc21
[B]   99-047364

Note to Parents and Teachers

The series Famous People in Transportation supports national social studies standards related to the ways technology has changed people's lives. This book describes the lives of Wilbur and Orville Wright and illustrates their contributions to transportation. The photographs support early readers in understanding the text. This book also introduces early readers to subject-specific vocabulary words, which are defined in the Words to Know section. Early readers may need assistance to read some words and to use the Table of Contents, Words to Know, Read More, Internet Sites, and Index/Word List sections of the book.

Table of Contents

Boyhood 5
Building Flying Machines 11
Flyer 17

Words to Know 22
Read More 23
Internet Sites 23
Index/Word List 24

Wilbur Wright was born in 1867. Orville Wright was born in 1871. The Wright brothers grew up in Dayton, Ohio. They liked to build kites.

Wilbur Wright

Orville Wright

6

Wilbur and Orville's father gave them a toy helicopter. Propellers helped the toy to fly. The brothers played with the toy. They built other toys like it.

The brothers opened a bicycle shop in Dayton in 1892. They sold and fixed bicycles. They also built bicycles.

10

Wilbur and Orville began
to build gliders in 1900.
Gliders are light planes that
use the wind to fly. The
brothers tested a glider at
Kitty Hawk, North Carolina.
They flew it as a kite.

The brothers watched how birds fly. Birds use their wings and the air. Wilbur and Orville learned how to build better wings. They flew new gliders at Kitty Hawk in 1901 and 1902.

14

The Wright brothers worked hard to make gliders fly farther. They tested more than 200 wing shapes.

The Wright brothers wanted to build an airplane that could power itself. They built a gasoline engine that turned two propellers. They put their engine on an airplane. They named the airplane the *Flyer.*

Orville flew the *Flyer* at Kitty Hawk in 1903. The airplane traveled 40 yards (37 meters). Wilbur later flew the *Flyer* 284 yards (260 meters).

Wilbur Wright died in 1912. Orville Wright died in 1948. The Wright brothers' work led to the invention of modern airplanes.

Words to Know

engine—a machine that changes an energy source into movement; the engine on the *Flyer* changed energy from gasoline into movement.

experiment—to plan to try something new; the Wright brothers experimented with many types of wings before building the *Flyer*.

glider—a light aircraft that flies by coasting on the wind; a glider has no engine or power source.

helicopter—an aircraft with large rotating blades on top; the blades move in a circle to make the helicopter fly; Orville and Wilbur played with a toy like a helicopter; it was made of paper, cork, and a rubber band.

machine—a tool made of moving parts that is used to do a job

propeller—a set of turning blades that move an airplane through the air

AGAINST THE STORM

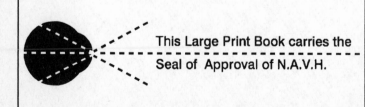

This Large Print Book carries the
Seal of Approval of N.A.V.H.